DRAMATIS PERSONAE

Life's isn't about finding yourself but creating yourself.

CHANDREYEE NASKAR

NewDelhi • London

BLUEROSE PUBLISHERS
India | U.K.

Copyright © Chandreyee Naskar 2024

All rights reserved by author. No part of this publication may be reproduced, stored in a retrieval system or transmitted in any form or by any means, electronic, mechanical, photocopying, recording or otherwise, without the prior permission of the author. Although every precaution has been taken to verify the accuracy of the information contained herein, the publisher assumes no responsibility for any errors or omissions. No liability is assumed for damages that may result from the use of information contained within.

BlueRose Publishers takes no responsibility for any damages, losses, or liabilities that may arise from the use or misuse of the information, products, or services provided in this publication.

For permissions requests or inquiries regarding this publication, please contact:

BLUEROSE PUBLISHERS
www.BlueRoseONE.com
info@bluerosepublishers.com
+91 8882 898 898
+4407342408967

ISBN: 978-93-6452-678-4

Cover design: Shivani
Typesetting: Sagar

First Edition: August 2024

Contents

Introduction 1

My Aim Behind Writing This Book 4

Discover Your Inner Treasury 5

Identify Your Inner Self 9

Stride Towards Success 14

Advance with a Sense Of Purpose 19

Enhance Your Perspective 24

Tame Your Aggressiveness 29

Master Leadership Skills 34

Develop Tiny Habits 39

Be Resilient to Judgements 44

Learn The Mystique of Generational Gaps 48

Develop Inner Strength 53

Resist the Downward Pull 56

Practice Empathy 60

Deciphering Concealed Characters 64

Change Your Perspective of Death 68

Acknowledgement 72

Introduction

As we proceed with the journey of our lives from the darkness of the womb to the womb of darkness, what does obsess us is the smorgasbord of individuals who foment trouble and prove to be the harbingers of difficulty in our lives. Some of these individuals are leaders or bosses, some are colleagues, and some are peers. The point of commonality of these individuals is that, they are by and large, maestro at playing on our emotions. Oftener than not, they appear endearing and refreshingly confident, radiating with ideas and enthusiasm and we fall under their spell. Only when it is too late do we discover that their confidence is irrational and their ideas ill-conceived. Among colleagues, they can be those who sabotage our work or careers out of surreptitious envy, overwhelmed to bring us down. On the other side, they can be colleagues, who reveal to our dismay, that they are completely out for themselves, using us as stepping stones.

What inevitably happens in these situations is that we are caught off guard, not expecting such behaviour. Often these types will hit us with elaborate cover stories to justify their actions. They are masters at bewildering us and alluring us into a drama they control. We might become infuriated, but at the end we feel rather desolate, the damage is already done. Then another individual enters our life and the same story repeats itself.

A similar sensation of confusion and desolation arises even when it comes to our own behaviour. For instance, we sometimes, without having a proper understanding of, or without quite picturing the logistics of it, we unleash words which packed a fierce potency. We are not quite sure, where it came from, but we are frustrated to find that some anger and tension from within has leaked out in a way which we later regret.

Under these circumstances, we consider ourselves getting enticed in self-destructive patterns that we cannot appear to be in charge of. It seems as if we foster an alien within ourselves who operates independent of our will power and drives us into doing the wrong things.

When we ponder upon these two things – others' hideous actions and our occasionally astonishing behaviour – the conventional conclusion that we arrive at – is that we usually have no clue as to what causes them. In order to avert the same pattern from reiterating, we need a profound understanding of it's root cause. The truth is that we humans, live on the surface, reciprocating emotionally to what people say and do. We cultivate opinions of others and ourselves that are rather simplified and lucid. We appear to live our entire lives with little or no awareness of our feelings and those around us.

Having such clarity about ourselves and those around us could change the course of our lives in ways more than one. An illustrated comprehension of characters of people we invariably deal with in our daily lives informs us about a person's actions, decisions and also indicates their motivations and goals. From daily life clamour to fierce competition in workplace or alma mater, understanding ourselves and others can have a positive impact. As the human population continues to burgeon, it is now becoming more critical than ever to make an effort to develop harmonious relationships. Though conflict is inevitable and understanding human behaviour would not necessarily remove it, with deeper awareness we can decipher ways to address problems more constructively and compassionately and save ourselves from the scourge of malice and heinous acts of sabotage.

When we become capable of excavating the true nature of other's characters and those of ours out from the depths of oblivion, we can be benefitted in a multitude of ways, from advancing our career and achieving goals to developing relationships and growing our professional network. This can help us to make decisions that align with our values.

My Aim Behind Writing This Book

The imminent entrepreneur Naval Ravikant once illustrated, "To write a great book, you must first become the book." I originally learned about the ideas mentioned here not necessarily because I had to live them in some point of my life or other but because I have seen others around me living those.

In the pages that follow, I have tried to put my heart and soul to present to you the scarce amount of wisdom that I have acquitted through my personal experiences and also from some science-supported researches. What I have tried to offer you is a synthesis of most compelling scientific discoveries and some of the best ideas of eminent personalities in the aforementioned regard which, I hope, will benefit you. If you find anything wise in these pages, you should credit to the many experts who have shared their humongous multitude of knowledge with the common people through the digital or printing media. If you find anything foolish, assume it my error.

I sincerely seek your forgiveness for any error I may have made in this book.

Discover Your Inner Treasury

"You have a treasure within you that is infinitely greater than anything the world can offer."

Eckhart Tolle

We humans possess an unfathomable quantum of riches within ourselves, which we will behold once we unfurl our psychogenic eyes. Since the treasury house is within us, we need to look within for the answer to our heart's desire. There is a gold mine within each of us from which we can derive everything we need to live a bounteous, joyful and illustrious life.

More than majority of the masses are utterly oblivious to the presence of this gold mine of peerless brilliance and eternal calibre within themselves. Whatever we desire of, we can extract therefrom. As the saying goes, "A magnetized piece of steel will lift about twelve times it's own weight, and if the same piece of steel is demagnetized, it will not even lift a feather". Similarly, we humans are of two types: One is the magnetized individual who is bursting of self-worth and assurance. They know their potential and firmly believe that they will realize it to their fullest. Then, there is the demagnetized one. They are defined by self-doubt, fear for rejection or criticism and apprehensions. Their lingering insecurities always impede them from seizing the opportunities that come their way. This type of man will not get very far in life because, if they are intimidated to move forward, they will merely remain where they are.

If you want to choose to be the magnetized man, then what you undeniably need to do is realize your latent powers maximally to lure more gratification and bounty to your lives. Unveiling your true potential requires self-awareness, self-belief, and a commitment to personal development. By embracing self-awareness, setting clear goals, and cultivating a positive frame of mind, you can unlock your full capabilities and live a more fulfilling and empowered life full of opportunities that come tapping into your authentic self. You should also bear in mind that the path to realizing your true potential is enduring and requires utmost resilience, support and adaptability. You should be kind to yourself, stay dedicated, and be prepared to adjust your approach when necessary to fully harness your talents and potential.

All you need to do is commingle your mental and emotional forces with the virtuousness you wish to embody, and your mind will reciprocate correspondingly.

"Find the place inside yourself where nothing is impossible."

Deepak Chopra

The more you think of yourself as worthless, stupid, or ugly, the more you get trapped in a labyrinth weaved out of your own menacing thoughts. The same is applied to our perspective of others. The more you delve yourself into the habit of seeing people as stubborn, selfish more you condition yourself to interpret life that way. You get to see more of those kind of people everywhere.

To sum up, every individual has his or her potential to achieve success in their own manner, no matter how large or small that achievement may seem to the world. Then, if successful and unsuccessful people both have that inherent potential within themselves to succeed, what is that which separates the successful people from the unsuccessful ones? The explanation is as follows: the successful ones are capable of calling their inherent forces into action whenever the need arises and making use of them to the fullest. They are always found to be giving maximum output in minimum resources. They use their resources- skills, knowledge or finances in the best possible way and always try to learn more efficient ways to enhance their utilization.

If you too want to make the most of your gifted life by being successful in our respective way, the first and foremost thing you need to do is to recognize your particular inclinations and then acuminate your skills to advance towards them with unflinching self-faith. You should know everything around outside you is temporary. May be people around you can make you feel good or bad sometimes but at the end, you should be confident enough to reach your goal that will bring you happiness galore. Here, I would like to emphasise that you take care not to mentally box yourself into a narrow version of happiness. It is unlikely that your actual path through life will match the exact journey you had in mind when you set off. It makes no sense to restrict your happiness when there are many paths to success.

You should not expect anything from anyone and even if you get something, try to interpret it as an aloft bliss. This will give you unexpected gratification. Conversely, if you have some expectations and those are not fulfilled, you will become morose and gloomy. Thus, if you expect nothing from somebody, you are never disappointed.

"When you have expectations, you are setting yourself up for disappointment."

Ryan Reynolds

Identify Your Inner Self

We all are quite acquainted with the helplessness and misery we go through when anything goes wrong in our life. The moment we humans are aware of how our emotions operate and dominate us is the moment they lose their hold on us and can be tamed. For this purpose, we need to ponder upon how we react or operate under stress. We need to reflect upon our decisions, especially those which have been ineffective, to find out and scrutinize what did not work. We need to look at our strengths and weaknesses. We must know our uniqueness- what sets us apart from others. This will eventually direct us into a path that is in alignment with our uniqueness and quest in life; and ultimately to success.

We should stop listening so much to the words and opinions of others, telling ourselves who we are. We should question what we think and why we feel a certain way. We need to know ourselves thoroughly- our innate tastes and inclinations, that spheres that inherently attract us. We should work every day on improving the skills that correlate with our unique spirit and reflect our uniqueness. We must open-heartedly embrace what makes us different.

Emotions are the lifeblood of human experience. They are the driving forces that forge our decisions, actions and reactions. Whether it is passionate love that calls for conjugal bliss or the rage that results in a riot or war- emotions are at the ultimate core of what calls us to action. So, having a profound understanding of our emotions is necessary for enhancing the quality of our life. By harnessing the powers of our emotions, we become architects of our destiny.

If you too want to tame your emotions and enforce them productively, they first and foremost thing you need to do is identify your emotions.

Once identified, immediately acknowledge the value of the emotion and try to decipher what it is trying to convey. At the most basic level, it tries to signal that something must change.

We need to question our inner self how we want to feel and what would make us feel that way right now. We also need to ask ourselves how we interpret the situation we presently are in- what we admire about it and what we detest about it and what it has been teaching us. Learning how a problem occurred will help us prevent it from recurring and helps us to interpret every problem as a gift.

At times, think back to a specific time when you successfully dealt with a similar emotion and how you had triumphed over it. Relieve the moment as a come back story and let the confidence wash over you. Reminiscing our triumphant moments lends powerful reassurance that you will navigate through this emotion once more.

Strengthen your vision of how you will handle this difficult emotion by imagining several strategies that help you experience the emotion you want to feel. If one doesn't work, try another. Rehearse until you feel certain you can deal with the emotion.

Do something right away that shows you can master your emotions. Express the emotion in a healthy way that reinforces what you rehearsed and changes the way you feel. Remember, you always had a choice when it comes to mastering your emotions and it all begins with the steps you take now.

Every emotion is an action signal. It's your body's way of communicating with you. But sometimes it is challenging to determine the precise message.

If you feel:

Discomfort: change your state, clarify what you want and advance in that direction.

Fear: prepare yourself to deal with an upcoming event to avoid negative consequences.

Hurt: unmet expectations resulted in a perceived loss. It signals an opportunity to grow by improving your communication next time.

Anger: an important rule or standard was violated. Clarify your standard and realize that others may not share that same standard.

Frustration: change your approach until you reach your desired outcome.

Disappointment: an expectation was unrealistic. Adjust your goals or expectations to be more accurate.

Guilt: you violated your own standard. Take actions to make things right and ensure it would not happen again.

Inadequacy: level up your game to get better in this area. For example, practice the underlying skills more.

Overwhelmed: you are doing too much at once. Identify what is a priority, rank them, and make progress on what is important.

Loneliness: you have an unmet need for connection. Identify the type of connection and take action toward it.

To truly master your emotions and gain a deep sense of emotional meaning, we must proactively nurture the positive emotions we want to feel. Whether it is more love and warmth or more drive and unshakable confidence, the best way to strengthen them is through habitual practice.

When you have already gained some confidence brainstorming your more positive qualities, then give yourself the time to face your weaknesses. Everyone has a combination of good and bad qualities, so don't let shame hold you back. The process isn't about self-deprecation or self-criticism but to notice where to lay emphasis on to become the best version of oneself.

Once you have made the list, choose a trait you would like to focus on improving. Focus on smaller, more easily adjustable traits that contribute to larger ones. For instance, if you want to improve your agreeableness, you might begin by becoming more easy-going.

The best way to overcome a negative emotion is to practice it's opposite. If you are irascible, look at composed individuals and try to understand their behaviour while confronting a similar situation. When it comes to impatience, short-temperedness, irascibility (these are some of the staunchest problems of youngsters today)- incorporating tranquilizing practices like yoga, journaling and meditation into your daily regimen can be utmost beneficiary as these remind you to slow down and appreciate the moment.

The starting point of authority is deciphering your strengths and weaknesses, those which you are in cognizance of and those which you are oblivious to. It resonates with what Aristotle rightly demonstrated, "Knowing yourself is the beginning of all wisdom."

Stride Towards Success

Success is all about growing as a person, making a difference in your world, continuously learning, tackling challenges head-on, and pushing your boundaries. This journey brings with it a profound sense of achievement and self-fulfilment, which contributes significantly to our overall happiness in life. Therefore, with this perception that success brings happiness, everyone seems to be chasing it.

Whenever in life, we humans embark on a journey with a definite goal, we come to terms with the reality that getting what we want is rarely easy. Success with depend largely on a lot of sincere effort and some luck. In the process, even if we fail to accomplish what we desired of, we will have to scrutinize meticulously what we did wrong and yearn to learn from the experience.

If you really strive to get something, you need to embed in your mind the fact that you need to earn it with enough effort, unflinching and unswerving focus, and sheer dedication. You should also make you believe yourself that no task is impossible if pursued with the aforementioned facets. With such a realistic attitude, you can muster up the requisite patience and begin work. "If you wish to succeed in life, make perseverance your bosom friend, experience your wise counsellor, caution your elder brother and hope your guardian genius", said Joseph Addison. People possessing these qualities succeed in whatever they might endeavour, while others bear the ignominy of failure in almost every activity they indulge in. Success, therefore does not come out of the blue; perseverance, experience, meticulousness, unswerving determination- all amalgamate together as the driving force behind it.

Celebrated personalities who have left their footprints in the sands of time for hundreds of thousands of individuals to follow, besides hard work and perseverance, also possessed a keen and sharp mind with a clear vision of the goal they want to attain in life. This ambition acted like a beacon of light, impelling them to relentlessly strive towards their goal. They also had the courage of conviction to move away from the beaten track and blaze a new trail for others to follow.

Alongside the aforementioned qualities, you must exercise caution and patience while dealing with problems. Just as a rolling stone gathers no moss, similarly, rushing from one action to another without reflecting upon it's implication gets one nowhere. There is, therefore, need for pondering immaculately, seeking the views of elders and peers before taking a decision. Decision once taken must be implemented patiently because all good things take time to happen.

The last but not the least prerequisite is a positive frame of mind and outlook as this is the tool which enables one to exhibit an optimistic approach to problems and seek opportunities in them.

"Life's battle does not always go, to the stronger and the fastest man, but sooner or later the man who wins is the man who thinks he can."

H.W. Longfellow

Any success that you achieve in life inevitably depends on some fortunate timing, the contributions of others, the educators who held your hand firmly along the way through darkness; and of course a lot of sincere effort from your part. Whenever we humans feel that we have made an accomplishment we had striven for, we inherently tend to forget all of these and assume that any success stems from our superior self. We begin to assume our grandiosity and imagine we have that golden touch and that we can mystically transform our skills to some other medium. We grow distant from those who had helped us, seeing them as stepping stones. It is an inherent nature of grandiosity to alter our perception of reality and makes it awfully hard to have an accurate assessment of ourselves. This makes us oblivious to the perils that this sensation of grandiosity is causing to us. It may cause us to overestimate our own skills and underestimate the obstacles that we had to overcome so painstakingly. If the scenario appears like this, our grandiosity will impede us from learning from our experiences and developing ourselves, because we are engulfed by the assumption that we are already large and great.

To keep yourself ever ascending the stairs of success, you need to identify the signs of grandiosity in yourself and learn not only how to manage those but also how to canalize this energy into a productive one.

Your aim with grandiosity should be to continually look for challenges just above your skill level. If the projects you attempt are below or at your skill level, you will become easily bored and your focus will begin to dissipate. If they are far above the level you are acquainted with, you will be more prone to failures, thus, eventually rendering your confidence macerated. However, if they are calibrated to be more challenging than the last project, but to a moderate degree, you will find yourself more vitalized. If you direct yourself in this direction, your focus will gradually rise as well. This is the optimum path toward learning. If you fail, you will not feel harried but will seize the experience as an opportunity to learn even more. If you succeed, your confidence will increase but this will not arouse an unhealthy feeling of superiority.

But that which is instrumental for your sublime enlightenment is to analyse the components after any kind of success. Realizing that the element of luck is inevitably there, as well as the role that the mentors played in your fortune, will neutralise the tendency to inflate your powers. You should always bear in mind, the fact that success and complacency walk hand in hand. You need to learn to pay less attention to the applause, which grows louder with successive bouts of success; and be circumspect of impertinence with your growing sense of superiority – for you will need your allies. The power that will be built organically, by consolidating and concentrating our forces; with your feet deeply rooted to the ground; will be more real and enduring.

Remember; "The gods are merciless, while those who fly too high on the wings of grandiosity; and they will make you pay the price."

Advance with a Sense of Purpose

There is nothing more disorienting and distressing than to witness our years in life pass by without a sense of direction, grasping to reach goals that keep swerving, and squandering our youthful energies. We are obligated to face this aforementioned predicament, if we advance in life without any unflinching sense of purpose.

In today's world where the competition is fierce and the competitors inexorable, we face a particular predicament: no sooner does our schooling end than we find ourselves, all of a sudden, entangled in the ruthless work world. Only a few years before, if we were fortunate, our parents formed a protective shield around us and were there to direct us. Now we find ourselves on our own with negligible or no life experience to rely upon. We have to make decisions and choices that will affect our entire future.

In the not so distant past, people's life and career choices were somewhat limited. They would settle into the particular jobs or roles that were available to them and adhere to those for decades.

But such durability is elusive today, as the world changes more exponentially than ever. Everyone is caught up in the relentless struggle to make it; people have never been so preoccupied with their needs and agendas. Veneering this unprecedented state of affairs, we tend to react in either of the following ways.

Some of us, excited by all the changes and the prospects they bring along, actually embrace the new possibilities. The potpourri of opportunities offered by the digital world dazzles us. We enthusiastically experiment, try many different jobs, get involved into different relationships and contingencies. Commitments to a single career or person feel like unnecessary restrictions on our freedom. Obeying orders and adhering to authority figures seem antiquated. Finally, we arrive at that façade of life where we figure out what to do with our lives; and our main motivation becomes – to take our lives where we please.

Some of us, however, react the antithetical way: Frightened of the clamour, we hastily opt for a career that is pragmatic. WE settle on a salient relationship. What motivates us to establish that stability that is too difficult to find in this world.

Both paths, nevertheless, tend to lead to some problems further along the way. In the first case, trying so many things out, we hardly develop proficiency in one particular demesne. We might now covet a relationship that is perpetual; but we have not inculcated within ourselves the virtue of forbearance. Further the thoughts of restrictions to our freedom that a lasting relationship will present, aggravates the scenario.

In the second case, the career we devoted ourselves to in the distant past, might begin to seem defunct and life demands an exhilarating freshness. This is when we might start to feel increasingly tempted by the salmagundi of possibilities in the modern world.

As life goes on, we start to find stints of frustration that are to severe to repress; we are gnawed by the anxiety that comes with living below our potential.

It is then when, we, without any solid accomplishments, begin to be acquainted with the discrepancy between our dreams and reality. Our skills stagnate and our potential dissipates; and we seem to be engulfed by an eerie sensation of insecurity.

Providentially, there is one way out of this predicament and this compass and guidance system, is by nature, available to each and every one of us.

When we delve into this eternal guidance system, all of the negative emotions that besiege us in our aimlessness are neutralized and even get transformed into positive ones. With a sense of direction, in the form of an overall career path that entangles with our particular inclinations; we have a calling in life.

This path does not require that we follow one straight line, or that our inclinations be narrowly focused. The path involves mastering a kaleidoscope of skills and amalgamating them in highly innovative and creative ways.

With a sense of purpose, we have an overall sense of our potential, hence we feel much less insecure. Devoting ourselves to the work that best suits our personalities, we develop am eternal resiliency; and know our self-worth and this self-awareness becomes our anchor in life.

With this guidance system in place, we can transform anxiety and stress into productive emotions. In trying to reach our goals, we are inevitably bound to manage a large quantum of anxiety and insecurities. If we have a compass and guidance system to direct our path and ventilate to us how far we have to go, we might feel quite relieved and submerged with positive emotions. In the process, we develop an important life skill: the ability to regulate our anxiety and stress levels. This knowledge or life skill can improve our health as well.

The moment we realize our life's work and work towards exploiting it to the fullest, we experience a mystical sensation of great fulfilment, of being lifted above the paltriness that so often marks daily life in the conventional world. We feel that we are contributing to something much larger than ourselves, and this ennobles us. We have accomplished that which will outlive us, and we are much far from that devitalizing feeling of having wasted our potential. To summarize, the need for purpose has a gravitational pull that no one can resist.

We should bear in mind that our contributions may come in many forms. Everyone does not necessarily have to be a colossal figure on the world's stage. We can do just well operating as a single person in a group, or running our own organization; as long as we retain a strong point of view that is our own and utilize this to delicately exert our influence. What matters is that it be tied to a personal need and inclination, and that our energy elevates us toward improvement and continual learning from experience.

Finally, we will surpass many individuals who are aimlessly meandering in this world, and ultimately recognize ourselves destined for greatness.

Enhance Your Perspective

We humans like to imagine that we have an objective knowledge of the world. This knowledge is particular to each and every individual. No two people see or experience the world in a similar way. Each of us views the world through a specific meniscus that fabricates and lends hue to our perception. Psychologists call this meniscus or lens our perspective. 'Perspective' can be defined as a way of feeling or acting toward a person, thing or situation.

We humans, by nature, seem to be most impressed by what we see and hear in the present in our immediate environment; which drives us into making decisions or behaving in manners which we later regret. For instance, we easily get carried away by enticing advertisements and make ourselves susceptible to alluring schemes that promise superfast results and quick money.

In the course of a day, our minds respond to a multitude of stimuli in the environment. Depending on our psychological composition, we tend to evaluate an object of thought. We, by our inherent nature, seem to be most impressed by what we see and hear in the present. In other words, we experience a narrowness of vision or short-sightedness. With this short-sightedness, we entangle ourselves with those who cannot see the consequences of their actions. In order to save ourselves from the unwelcome consequences of our narrowness of vision, we need to develop a far-sighted façade to our personality.

Almost all of us have experienced something similar to the following scenarios: we face a problem, and so we decide upon a strategy and take a seemingly appropriate initiative. We get overly frustrated when things do not go as we had planned. Or a person enters our life, and beguiled by his or her charm or enthusiasm, we become friends.

Then days go by and circumstances force us to reflect upon what had happened and how we had reacted. As we introspect, revelations come at the forefront. We realize that the problem we tried to solve was not really so grave and that we had aggravated the situation by hastily resorting to inappropriate decisions. We should have looked before we had leapt. And the new comrade ends up unveiling, to our dismay, his or her true self, that they are completely out for themselves, using us as stepping-stones. Upon sincere retrospection, we see that it is our impatience and our tendency to overreact which lands us in such helpless situations.

What this indicates at is that in the present moment we always find ourselves in dearth of foresight. With the passage of time, we discover that what was unobtrusive to us in the present now becomes obtrusive in retrospect. The emotions we felt in the present are no longer so strong; we can abdicate those emotionally and present ourselves with a panoramic view towards things. The further we ascend with the passage of time, the clearer view of things we exhibit. We learn to corroborate the fact time and time again, that time is the greatest teacher of all.

The aforementioned illustrations again reinforce the fact that most people live on the surface of the moment. They tend to overreact and panic at the face of any adverse situation for they can only see a narrow part of the reality. They are incompetent to entertain alternative ideas. Those who maintain their presence of mind and heighten their perspective above the immediate moment unleash their visionary powers and set themselves apart from the common individuals.

The first and foremost step that you must implement in order to become far-sighted is to train yourself to continually detach from the rush of events and elevate your perspective. A limited perspective can impede you from considering all aspects of a situation. Divulge out of your immediate stupor and zoom out and try to see the bigger picture.

Some issues deserve your attention. Others are meagre distractions that keep you from focusing on your daily chores and doing your best work. An elevation of perspective could mean filtering that which are worth worrying about and learning how to let things go.

Ask yourself what the consequences would be to let a situation go instead of being confrontational or ruminating on the negative. If they are insignificant, chances are that engaging with this minor upset will only consume energy you could channel into something more productive or enjoyable.

You need to encourage reflection, either before or after a situation that made you question your perspective and then, see what upsides and insides you gather. You should make it a point to slow down your thoughts by reflecting on the situation at hand instead of jumping to conclusions.

Most individuals live within a quite narrow dimension of time. It is our general tendency to associate the passage of time with something negative- aging and moving nearer to impending death. When it comes to future planning, we may try to think about our plans a year or two from now, but our thinking shares utmost resemblance with a trance, a mere desire, without any deep evaluation. In relation to the past we may have a few fine or unpleasant reminiscences from childhood and later years, but in general the past bemuses us.

In order to live a more rewarding life, we should learn to not see the passage of time as a foe but rather as a great pal; and embrace the infinite smorgasbord of perspective that it brings forth.

Though we should enjoy the present, we should learn to continually detach ourselves from the immediate rush of events and upraise our perspective. We should refrain ourselves from merely reacting and try to have a broader view of the context. Though the aforementioned sanity seems to be easy to acquire, it is really not so. These powers do not come naturally. These are acquired when shrewd expertise coincides with elevated wisdom.

Tame Your Aggressiveness

We humans like to imagine ourselves as peaceful species at heart. Being socialized animals, we convince ourselves to be loyal and accommodating to the society we belong to. But, more than often we behave in ways, rather aggressive ways that are in strict contradiction with this self-conceit. Some of the most potent causes of such aggressive behaviour may be financial distress, insecurities in workplace, or emotional jeopardy in an intimate relationship. Or perhaps it occurred under some circumstances when we found our prestige or that of our family at stake; or perhaps it arose when we felt particularly frustrated when we believed we were not getting the attention and recognition that we deserved. Memories of traumatic or exasperating events can also trigger aggressive feelings.

Aggression is a tendency that is inherent in every single human individual. There are some individuals whose lure for power and money and impatience to obtain it far surpass that of others. They turn particularly aggressive, being restless and even ready to resort to dishonourable or unjust means to get what they are running after. So, you need to understand and recognize these aggressors who are deleterious to society and be extra wary around them. And when it comes to your own aggressive nature, learn to harness and channelize that energy for purposes that will be high-yielding in the long run- voicing your opinion valorously, realizing your true potential and calling in life, standing up for those in need.

At some point of your life, you must come across people showing signs of frustration even at the slightest hint of an unpleasant situation. In such cases, in order to prevent physical or emotional harm, it is necessary to make an assessment and take measures to impede the situation from snowballing.

The first crucial step to save the fury from escalating is maintain your composer and listening to the aggressor as respectfully as possible. When aggressive people feel respected, they are likely to act less draconian. When you demonstrate that you empathize and understand how they feel, they are more likely to calm down and cooperate with you.

While it can be easy to stereotype an angry person and judge them accordingly, the same can affect your interaction with them. Stereotyping can hinder your understanding of their problem and situation.

Like everyone else, aggressors also deserve a chance. As mentioned earlier, you need to listen to what they want to say and acknowledge their opinion, if they are wrong, kindly explain it to them. Some aggressors are seen to calm down significantly when given respect.

And remember, if a difficult person is acting aggressively, there might be something triggering this behaviour. Giving them the benefit of doubt is sometimes all you need to clear the situation.

There are some people who are really more "hot-headed" than others are; their volatility and intensity of aggression is more than the average person, who refuse to listen to you and go on pouring ire and frustration and make it impossible to speak to them, thus, exacerbating the situation.

Under such circumstances, there is no point in speaking and the best thing to do would be to stay silent and wait for the right time to share your thoughts. By avoiding descending to their level, you take the high ground and can help solve the problem when the situation appears to calm down.

It is a characteristic trait of aggressive people to hate being told what to do. They rarely calm down when you tell them to do so. To the contrary, they grow increasingly irascible when they are being asked to calm down.

So, instead of demanding them to relax, ask them about their reason for being upset and how you can offer help. On cultivating a friendly and open line of communication, you can encourage the other party to express their frustrations without resorting to aggression. It is better to have a conversation that will procure results rather than that which will make the situation worse.

Though dealing with people is never easy, you should learn the skills it demands in order to save yourself or your near and dear ones from the scourge of aggressive people and the belligerent situations they act as an impetus for.

When it comes to your characteristic aggressive nature, the first and foremost thing you need to do is stop denying the reality of your own aggressive tendencies. Like all of us, you too exude aggression at certain moments of your life.

Now, your goal is not to repress this assertive energy but to become aware of it and learn to control and direct it so that both your emotional feelings and the psychological arousal that aggression causes, can be substantially reduced.

Whenever at any particular bellicose situation, you experience an extreme swell of aggressive emotions from your inner-self, before anything else, try to calm down inside. This involves controlling your outward behaviour and controlling your internal responses, taking steps to lower your heart rate, calm yourself down, and let the feelings subside.

An important step towards managing your aggressive nature is restructuring your perspective. In simpler words, you need to change the way you think. Whenever you tend to exude an upsurge of aggressiveness, ask yourself whether your emotions are rational. Your aggression may cause you to think in a very dramatic and overly exaggerated way, leading you to curse, swear, or speak in highly colourful terms. Instead, try replacing these thoughts with more rational ones. Through such reflection, you can unpack why you exhibit such behaviour and take steps to deconstruct those.

Also tell yourself that that particular misfortune or bellicosity is not the end of the world and reacting in an overly frustrated manner is not going to fix it anyhow.

In order to arrest your exodus of aggression, you need to put relaxation skills to work. Practice deep-breathing exercises, imagine a relaxing scene, or reiterate a calming word or phrase, such as "Everything's fine." You might also listen to music, write a journal or try a few yoga poses- whatever it takes to encourage relaxation.

Remind yourself time and again that showing aggressive behaviour is not going to fix anything and that it would not make you feel better (and may actually make you feel worse). Aggression can make you feel as though you are at the mercy of an unpredictable and powerful emotion, learn how to control it before it controls you.

Master Leadership Skills

We humans everywhere pursue power, prestige, and status. We want our verdict or command to be a driving force behind actions of many. We want to be acknowledged, recognized and applauded. History is replete with innumerable instances that reinforce the fact time and again that: a person with great power and status has access to more resources, worries less about survival, and proves to be living a more gratifying life.

From ancient times, we humans have been power seeking creatures at heart; we always strove for establishing our reserved authority upon our fellow beings. This is because high-status people (especially those in acquisition of a satrap's crown) enjoy the adulation, respect, and praise of others.

The essence of this authority that one longs for is that masses seek one's wisdom and choose one as their guiding light. In simple words, authority is the cornerstone of being a leader.

To acknowledge people of authority is not an admission of our inferiority but rather a simple acceptance of the need for such figures. Without leaders who direct us with much mental energy to our long-term solutions, we are lost in the labyrinth of life.

Now, as an impulse from your human nature, if you are desperate to establish authority, you should always bear in mind the fact that the core of authority is that people follow your lead, willingly. This resonates with eminent self-development author, Brian Tracy's virtuous words-"Become the leader that people would follow voluntarily, even if you had no title or position."

People of authority should not be seen as self-serving or narcissistic- in fact, those are the qualities that pose an ominous threat to their authority.

The foremost thing that you should yearn for if you aim at establishing authority is to devote yourself to earning people's respect and regard. Your authority will grow with each action that inspires respect and trust. The golden way to earning people's respect is by showing respect to them and their individual needs; as benevolence and empathy are critical to authority. Authority is more about responsibility towards others than power. The driving force behind you should not be lure for getting attention but bringing about the best possible results for the most people. Once you let your self-pride dissipate and absorb yourself in the work, you feel an unfathomably deep connection with your associates.

The more you avert your self-absorbed nature and deviate from your fantasies, the more you attune yourself to the needs of people; hence adapting accordingly to bring out new facets to captivate people.

Though eluded by false pride and exaggerated sense of self-conceit, you need to exude a certain degree of self-dignity and be happy with who you are. If you don't respect yourself, it is doubtful that others will. Moreover, self-respect helps you respect others.

We humans, by nature, appear to be locked in the moment. We are prone to overreacting and panicking, to seeing only a narrow part of the reality facing the group. We are devoid of any alternative ideas. But an exceptionally crucial prerequisite for fulfilling the true function of leadership is the presence of a third eye. Those who elevate their perspective and maintain their presence of mind at the face of any predicament, stand out as leaders. Hence, if you want to create an aura that others willingly follow, you need to cultivate a third eye for unforeseen forces and situations.

As a leader, you must be seen working as hard as or even harder than everyone else in the association body. Trust and confidence in your words and actions are crucial to your ability to lead others. You should not hesitate from making all the sacrifices that are necessary for your consistence, credibility and transparency. Then, your followers will try to subtly imitate you and internalize your values.

Presence is the most visible aspect of authority- how you stand, talk and walk bear contribute to the sense of presence you have around your followers. Hence, try to emphasize on your demeanour and concoct your personality traits into a charisma that people won't get over soon.

In a world full of endless distractions, you must focus profoundly on your work. Setting your eyes on our long- and short-term goals, you must remain concentrated and focused. Yearning for excellence, you should adhere to the highest standards of your work and place a premium value on effort. You need to try to develop a sense of personal mission- to embark on a journey that would in some way or the other contribute to the times you live in. Being compelled by such an inner authority, you would be able to resist all the impediments that life places in your path.

If you aspire to consolidate your power as a leader, you must show some initial toughness; if people get the impression early on that there is a delicate façade to their leader's character, they will try to surpass him or her. Your tone in speaking to or instructing them should be high-handed and undaunted. People always respect strength in their leader, unless it does not foment fears of the abuse of power. You will always have ample time to unveil your soft side, but if you start soft, you signal that you are feeble.

Remember when you get the opportunity to exercise authority, use it in a sagacious manner. Authority is more about responsibility towards others than power. Be generous to others, let your team take chances, let others stand out by getting opportunities of sharing their wisdom or knowledge. Mentor or coach those who you understand to be dedicated and hard-working and help them nurture their skills and cumulatively emerge as a formidable force.

While striving for power and authority, always bear in mind that: though the pursuit of wealth and power can be a source of motivation and innovation, it can also be a destructive force that perpetuates inequality and harm. Once you achieve the power you strove for, always remain humble. And value invariably all those who contributed to your journey to the crown.

"To handle yourself, use your head; to handle others, use your heart."

Eleanor Roosevelt

Develop Tiny Habits

It is too easy to overestimate the importance of one defining moment and underestimate the value of making small improvements on a daily basis. More than often, we tend to convince ourselves that enormous success is preceded by enormous action. Whether it is losing weight, winning a championship, developing academic prowess, or attaining any other goal, we pressurize ourselves to make some earth-shaking improvement that everyone will talk about.

In the meantime, we seem to be utmost oblivious to the gigantic results tiny, even apparently unnoticeable improvements can bring about. The difference a minuscule improvement can make over time is startling.

The power of tiny changes can be too difficult to cherish in daily life. We often dismiss small changes because they don't seem to matter very much in the moment. If you work out for a month in a row, you are still out of shape. If you practice maths for three long hours today, you are still imbecile at the subject. If you save a little money now, you are still now rich. We make a few changes, but the results never seem to come quickly and so we hastily slide back into our previous habits.

Unfortunately, the time-consuming pace of transformation also makes it too difficult to stick to new good habits.

Your outcomes are a lagging measure of your habits. If you want to predict where you will end up in life, all you have to do is trace the path of tiny gains or tiny losses, and see how your daily choices will compound ten or twenty years down the line.

All big things have, after all, small beginnings. The seed of every habit is a single, tiny decision. But the more the decision is reiterated, the stronger grows the habit. The task of breaking a bad habit is like uprooting a staunch weed within us. To the contrary, the task of developing a good habit is like striding tirelessly along a path made of concrete stones and thorns.

Time elucidates the dividing line between success and failure. Time will inevitable give you the compounded output of whatever you provide it with. Good habits make time your friend while bad ones transform it into your formidable foe.

Habits are like the building blocks of our lives, each one contributing to our overall development. Initially, these tiny routines seem insignificant, but soon they build on each other and pave way for such unexpectedly mammoth wins that are of such intensity that far outweighs the cost of their initial investment. Though small, such habits are of indomitable might. To sum up, a regular practice or routine that small and easy to do, can evolve as a harbinger of incredible power and success in the long run.

We often overlook opportunities for growth because they seem small or insignificant. But as the example of exponential growth shows, even a tiny amount can lead to huge results over time. To realize this potential, we need to be open to change and willing to experiment. This means trying new things, even if they seem unimportant at first. By doing so, we can create the conditions for success and set ourselves up for long time growth.

Here's an example. Let's say that you start an investment bank account with an opening balance of Rs.1.

Yes, you ask, which bank will accept that? Just take it for a hypothetical example.

Now, every day, for one month, make a deposit that doubles what is in the account. So, on day 1, you add Rs.1 for a total of Rs.2; on day 2, you add Rs.2 for a total of Rs.4, and so on.

It appears both simple and idiosyncratic. And yet, after just two weeks, or 15 days of doing this, your account would hold Rs.16,384. On keeping doing it for another 10 days, for a total of 25 days, and now, your bank balance is a whooping Rs.16,777,216. Yes, you read it right. That is nearly Rs.16 million.

That is the power of compounded growth. Isn't it bewildering and amazing at the same time? So, never underestimate the power of small changes.

Try to view your everyday habits or daily routine with the similar perspective. Tiny changes in our daily habits- incorporation of some small activities into or elimination of some small activities from our daily regimen can work wonders. Just like those spare coins on the sidewalk, these small things add up. And once the momentum gets established, your return will quickly surpass your initial investment.

Breakthrough moments are often the results of many previous seemingly small actions, which build up the potential required to unleash a massive change.

You should start with one change that takes the least amount of effort and is not painstaking. This will act as a source of energy and motivation to fuel future changes. For example, if you want to replace your unhealthy eating habits by a healthy one, start by improving one meal per day, focus on this for a few weeks, and then increase it to two meals a day. If you adhere to this pattern with unflinching consistency, after a certain period of time, you suddenly begin to see some changes in your body which were unimaginable when you started. You yourself would not be able to make out the magic which transformed your corpulent body into a good shape. But, in the process, if you grew restless and fretful with the slow pace of transformation and so you slide back to your previous routine, your desired results remain pie in the sky.

This again reinforces the fact that outcomes are a lagging measure of our habits and that we get what we repeat. Small changes often appear to make no difference until you cross a critical threshold. The most powerful outcomes of any process are always delayed. You need to understand that the fruit is the last thing to appear on a tree. Hence, you need to be patient.

Be Resilient to Judgements

From early on in life, since we are being weaned, we develop a protective sense of personal physical space that none should violate. As we grow older, these protective senses metamorphose into a feeling of self-worth – we should not live our lives in duress. We always find people scrutinising us and bombarding us with judgements, making us feel overly anxious, annoyed or insecure which can be sometimes menacing and deleterious to our psyche. In the face of such perils, all we need to do is to set up rigid boundaries around ourselves to keep out intruders. We should cultivate a more self-absorbed and defensive side to our personality – we have to nurture and acknowledge our own interests, since nobody else will. This power is instrumental to our survival in this ruthlessly competitive era.

Despite your best attempts to be compassionate, you will inevitably encounter judgemental people. These people are characterised by a sarcastic and demeaning attitude towards others, whether to their face or behind their back.

It may appear tempting to combat someone else's judgement towards you, but this strategy does not exhibit a realistic approach. Having a defensive reaction often causes them to intensify their efforts, which can result in an aggravated conflict. This may render you even more drained, insecure or morose.

Instead consider remaining calm and respond with a statement that clearly elucidates your opinion.

Dealing with judgement can be tough, especially when it is coming from a relative, peer or colleague. Learning to let words go by without taking them personally and feeling bad about them is an enormous shift, to be sure. It helps a lot to imagine in advance more such comments coming your way and practice new responses to family and friends who do not seem to understand what caregiving really entails. You do not need to be snarky or hostile. To the contrary, you can even be compassionate once you step aside from the verbal onslaught and focus on their desired outcomes- and yours! Remember that a judgemental person's words are a reflection of their own beliefs- and not you. Critical people criticize themselves more than anyone else, so the judgement they pass is not actually as much about you, as it is about themselves. Whenever you face a judgement, think for some time before your initial reaction and your response. If you give yourself time to think, you can process and let go of your anger before responding to judgemental words.

Make sure your sensitivity or emotional reaction does not make you the judger. Think about whether it really is judgemental and how can respond, before you rush in and judge them back!

Whenever you recognise a judgemental person in your life, the first step you can take towards saving yourself from getting emotionally drained is limit the time you spend in their company. Focus on filling your priceless time with emotionally healthy people who inspire you and make you feel good about yourself.

The key to shift through the noise to hear the potentially valuable message, and there may be more than one. Once you step out the emotional overload of feeling attacked, judged and criticized, there may be some ideas that are worth exploring further.

There is always a silver lining, even when dealing with difficult people. It may be easier for you to respond to a judgement when you have found a bright side or thought to be grateful. For instance, if you are having trouble with a co-worker, you can remind yourself that you at least have a job and be thankful for that. If a friend is judging you, think about your support system of other friends who can back you up. Think of each situation where you feel judged as a learning experience, judgement is inevitable at times because many people do it naturally. Every time you face it, you learn to deal with it more efficaciously. Even if your relationship with the judgemental person is damaged or cut off, you can be grateful that you stood up for yourself and took care of your personal needs.

Always remember that a judgemental opinion is not a fact. Remind yourself time and again that regardless of what other people think, you don't deserve to feel bitter or insecure about who you are. You don't need to depend on other people for happiness, least of all those judging you, their opinion does not affect your worth as a person. And always concentrate on living the moment. You will be most depressed when you obsess over the past or the future. On the other hand, when you let go of tantalizing worries and live firmly in the present, you are more likely to enjoy your life.

Remember that it is not your job to make a judgemental person change; your emotional well-being comes first. Standing up to someone who judges you is hard, and cutting them off can be harder, but you will be happier if you channelize your energy into more positive relationships. After dealing with a judgemental person, make it a point to talk it over with someone you trust with your whole heart. (for me that person has always been my mother ☺)

Judgemental people are everywhere, and you may be one of those people yourself! But instead of trying to fix or change everyone else, focus on what is in your control: your responses and actions. The more you dial those in, the less you will feel affected with other people. When confronted with criticisms and judgements, learning to respond in new ways takes practice, patience, perseverance and courage. Please be patient with yourself as you learn new strategies and coping skills.

Learn the Mystique of Generational Gaps

In our initial years of life, we are akin to a lump of clay, which can be moulded in conformity with the ideas of our parents and teachers. We seem to be going through a process of assimilating the strange new world we were cast into at birth. We learn language, certain essential values, ways of thinking, and how to function among people. Our minds are supremely open at this moment, and because of this our experiences are most intense and entangled with strong emotions.

Then, when we reach our teen years or perhaps earlier, we become aware that we belong to a generation of young people whom we can easily bond with as we learn the way we interpret the world is similar to the way they do.

In this phase, we inevitably go through a period of rebellion, as we often come to believe that the ideologies of our parents are not aptly fitting in our own experience of reality. What they have taught us seem to be irrelevant, and we crave for ideas that empathize more with our youthful perspective. This always gives rise to an underlying tension, accompanied by some hostility and bitterness. In any event, to some extent or the other, a clash and struggle inevitably takes place between two generations and their ideologies. The root antecedent of these antagonisms is believed to be the following: young people belonging to new generations try to create something more relevant to their experience of the world, something that appears to be in parity with their values, tastes, inclinations and spirit and that indelibly goes in a direction opposite to that of the previous generation.

Many of those belonging to the older generation insist on their own way of acting and contempt the youngsters as immature, restless, undisciplined, aggressive, overly pampered, benighted, et cetera. Since a generational perspective is formed among the youth, generations seem to be moving in an opposite direction to the previous generation. This trend may pave way for societal disparities, and we would asphyxiate ourselves with too much individualism or stagnation. If we want to keep us from this doom, we must recognize what seems to be an overall human spirit that transcends any particular boundaries set by time and that keeps us evolving.

Findings indicated that the older generations have had superior empathetic and societal abilities; and have had the opportunity to live through many different experiences and may have developed a sense of resilience and wisdom from those life experiences which the younger generation is yet to acquire. Therefore, there is much to be gained by looking at the world from the point of view of our parents, and adapting to some of their values. The same is implied to the older generation as well. People belonging to the older generation should not refrain from sharing the perspectives of their children for that will give them a sense of where the world is headed or what is going around the corner. This will help them to anticipate futuristic trends. Such a shared understanding will help us make better sense of the underlying changes going on in all areas of society, and exert a tranquilizing effect on us as we view all the events in the world with an elevated perspective.

First and foremost, we need to refashion our outlook towards the generation we belong to. We need to understand that feeling our generation is superior is simply an empty apparition. This profound understanding of the spirit of our generation should in no way be adulterated by our own emotions and prejudices. We should try to efficaciously engage ourselves in the inevitable process of making judgements of good or bad about our generation or the previous or next one, and let go of them.

It was in the years of our extreme youth that a particular spirit of our generation was instinctively ingrained within us. It is our inherent tendency to adhere to that spirit, that particular way of thinking, that particular way of behaving throughout our life; and anything dissimilar seems annoying. As we grow older, we hold on more tightly to the times we have left behind and stop evolving with our thinking.

But, that is not the right direction to follow. It is not that we should abandon the spirit that marked us. What we should do is to modernize our spirit, blending our thoughts and ideas with those of the younger generation that appeal to us. We should learn to update and incorporate the styles of both the past and the present generation in our perspective and way of acting. We often find a completely false notion lingering in our minds: that we are superior to those in the past and that the past means dead. The sooner we rid ourselves of such absurd and meaningless notions and ideas the better for our cumulative growth. We should never forget that most of all that we think and experience, all the luxuries we enjoy, our most usual beliefs and practises, are products of excruciating struggles of past generations.

We must try to learn from and educate ourselves with the wisdom latent in events that history is replete with; and inculcate within ourselves the spirit and valour of celebrated historical personalities. When we see the world through the eyes of valiant historical figures, interpreting it with our active imagination, we are unconsciously stepping towards an unimaginable door of opportunities. We need to inculcate some of the values and ideas of the past, which we find timeless and eternal within our thought process so that we can give the effect that what we are attempting in the present is a more perfect and progressive version of what had happened in the past.

Such a fashion of work will generate a ripple effect in the vicinity, as our work will appear to be beyond time itself.

Develop Inner Strength

"Character is like a tree and reputation it's shadow. The shadow is what we think of it; the tree is the real thing."

Abraham Lincoln

Character is an individual's unique combination of internalized beliefs and moral habits that motivates and forges how that individual relates to others and even to himself. The character influences significantly a person's career and life. Building a strong character is important for success in life for character is all about the core values we hold and how these values translate into actions. It is not just about what we do, but why we do it and how we do it consistently, especially when faced with adversity. Moreover, a person's character is reflected in how they treat others, especially in times of need. Character building fosters qualities such as empathy and compassion, enabling individuals to understand the feelings and perspectives of others. These qualities are instrumental for creating a more harmonious and inclusive society.

A strong character ensures that you achieve your potential. If you consistently act in accordance with a righteous code of moral conduct, people will find you more dependable and trustworthy, which will help you connect with people in your life who can help you achieve your goals.

The first step towards developing a strong character is being a promise-keeper. No matter how small the promise is, no matter to whom the promise is made, strive to keep your word. If events prevent you from honouring the commitment you made, get back to the people in concern and let them know why you could not fulfil your promise. Resolve to handle your word as a precious currency and watch how your value rises in everyone's eyes.

At the end of a certain span of time, get in the habit of going over the decisions you made. Are you content? Do your actions reflect positively on you as a person of character? What could you have done better? Every action we take, no matter how small, has our character stamp on it.

You should exhibit humility in achievement and success. Humility, under any circumstances, should never be run over. Humility is an embodiment of the knowledge that we are stronger together than apart. Humility is all about giving all we have and doing it again.

You need to try to be nice when everything tempts you not to be nice. A quiet strength of character exists in being humble and nice. Being nice does not mean low expectations. Too often, we want to play to the crowd and say outrageous things to incite or fit into one. Instead, we need to stand out by saying and doing things that are helpful.

Always get up, no matter what, to create something better than the day before. You will definitely get knocked down and stepped on. At the face of such situations, always remember the old political adage that, "What goes around, comes around." If someone is stepping on you, holding you back, or ignoring you, nature has a way of dealing with that, so focus on what you can do and do so with a strong sense of character. Secondly, keep getting up and giving life to what you are meant to create. After all, this is the only way your purpose will take root.

While pursuing your goals, always bear in mind the fact that laziness achieves nothing. Whatever your purpose may be, you need to do the work. When you do so, your character will show it's strength in purpose.

And always keep in mind that no task is too small, and no individual is too ordinary or extraordinary to extend a hand and help. Hence, never think or do things that make others feel looked down upon. Always pitch in, no matter how small or large the task may appear to be. Our hands are meant to be extended in a helpful way; it is why we have arms and elbows! We are designed to do the work, hug each other, and extent a helping hand.

How each of us builds our character may vary. The most important thing is to understand what builds character and then do those things as often as you can.

Resist the Downward Pull

We humans are herd animals. We are desperate to fit in, to bond with others, and to earn the respect and appraise of our peers. Our evolutionary history bears testimony to the aforementioned verisimilitude for our ancestors lived in tribes. Getting separated from the tribe- or worse, being excluded- was a sentence to death. "The lone wolf dies, but the pack survives."

For the time being, those who associated and fraternised with others enjoyed increased safety and access to resources. As a consequence, one of the deepest human desires is to belong and proximity exerts a powerful effect on our behaviour.

At certain moments in life, we humans may feel certain energies which are powerful, with sensations unlike any other; but these energies are something we really discuss or analyse. These feelings stem from a situation when we operate in groups of people. In the group setting, we feel different emotions, influenced by the group mood. When we find ourselves in large groups such as a cultural programme, a sports event, a congregation or a political gathering, it is impossible not to feel ourselves caught up in the medley of collective emotions. If we are on the right or the left, our opinions will almost always follow the same direction on numerous issues, as if drawn by some magical force, and yet very few of us would admit this influence on our thought patterns.

We humans being social animals to the core, abominate the feeling of isolation and find the sensation of belonging tremendously relieving. This intense desire to belong is stimulated by being in a group. Our automatic reactions in a group, or our propensity to imitate others, can be considered to collectively stem from a hardly comprehensible, physiological force called the "social force".

The "social force" is neither positive nor negative. It is just an anatomical figment of animal character which is prevalent in it's highest degree among humans. Our interpretation of this force dictates whether the force is an upward pull or a downward one.

For example, when we trace the dark chapters of history, we find those replete with portentous testimonies of untouchability, apartheid, communal riots, et cetera. In this regard, social force evolved as a downward pull. Further, with our technological prowess, they can be the source of our most violent and genocidal behaviour. To sum up, if social force, in any way, degrades our humaneness and rationality, we can say it exerts an ominous downward pull.

To the contrary, if social force promotes virtues such as compassion, cooperation and empathy, it undeniably exerts an upward pull. Examples of specialists working hand in hand to bring about a amelioration in any respective field, or a group of peasants, farmers, or any common men protesting with continual team spirit to emancipate their rights, all throw light upon the positive effects of social force.

The problem we face as social animals is not that we experience the force, but that we lack it's profound understanding. We become influence by others without realizing it. Accustomed to unconsciously following what others say and do, we lose our own capability to think for ourselves. When faced with critical decisions in life, we simply imitate what others or so called renowned personalities have done. This can pave way for many inappropriate decisions.

"Social forces" are like a double-edged sword. Their adverse effects can cut you down just as easily as their positive impacts can build you up, which is why comprehending the details is really necessary. We need to know how "social forces" work and how to design them to our respective liking, so that we can avoid the dangerous half of the blade.

If we want to keep ourselves from the adverse effects of social force, the first and foremost thing we need to do is to cultivate a thorough understanding of the effects that groups have on our psyche. With such awareness, we can repel the downward pull.

This way, we can develop ourselves into excellent social interactors, whose naturalness do not tend to offend the group values; while inwardly maintaining a necessary distance and some mental space to think for ourselves. With this degree of freedom, we can make decisions in life that are appropriate to who we are and our circumstances.

We must always come to the stolid conclusion that the primary group we belong to is that of the human race. We need to embrace this connotation whole heartedly and develop a deep sense of belonging, accepting ourselves as descendants of the same original humans.

Practice Empathy

Empathy is greater than anything a state of mind; it is an ability to take on another's perspective, to understand, feel, and possibly share and respond to their experience. It is a natural and most remarkable instrument for connecting to people and accomplishing societal power. Putting ourselves in another person's shoes might lead us to interact with compassion and do what we can to improve their situation. In doing so, we can be compelled to take action to lessen the other person's distress as well as that of our own. Having empathy enables us to build social connections. To feel connected to others is hugely important for our optimal well-being. It is the very basis of human relationships and helps us to feel valued, loved, and cared for. Being connected to others is extremely crucial for our mental well-being.

However, this tool is blunted by our inherent self-absorption or narcissism. Since we humans are social animals to the core, our psychological drive makes us feel a never-ending need for attention. Those individuals who exude self-absorption and solipsism to an unfathomable degree, can be broadly categorized into a class of "deep narcissists". Deep narcissists become so thoroughly self-absorbed that they find it utterly difficult to restore normalcy back to themselves; and constant attention becomes their only way of survival.

In order to live a coherent and balanced life, the first and foremost thing we need to do is to be honest about our own nature and accept it gracefully but try to incorporate some delicate yet instrumental changes. We should develop a strong and benign self-esteem; and love ourselves to a degree that is healthy, both for ourselves and those in the vicinity.

Once we identify our true nature, we must begin to make the transformation into the "healthy narcissist". Healthy narcissists possess a positive sense of self that is in alignment with the greater good. Healthy narcissists reflect an abundance of self-enhancing features and a relative absence of other-derogating elements. They exhibit a resilient nature; hence recover more quickly from any wounds or insults. They do not rely upon validation from others. They realize their shortcomings and flaws and work harder to overcome those. In innumerable ways, they appear to embrace their authentic self, their self-love is more real and organic. Since they tend to direct their focus towards work more intensely, they, more than often, tend to be successful in their ventures.

The other component of character of healthy narcissists is that they exhibit empathetic values. This need to create empathy is an extremely crucial step towards peaceful co-existence. Empathy creates its own upward, positive momentum.

Researches show that having a strong social support system tends to increase one's happiness. Having empathy enables us to build social connections. To feel connected to others is hugely important for our optimal wellbeing. It is the very basis of human relationships and helps us to feel valued, loved and cared for. Being connected to others is good for our mental wellbeing. Empathy plays a pivotal role in building successful interpersonal relationships of all types: in the family unit, workplace and beyond. Lack of empathy, therefore, is one indication of conditions like antisocial personality disorder and narcissistic personality disorder.

In some circumstances, its natural to feel low empathy. It is natural to have a hard time empathizing with someone who bullied us or mistreated our loved ones. This could be entirely attributed to the situation and not reflective of how well we truly empathize with people in general.

Empathy, like any other trait, is subject to both atrophy and development. Enhancing our listening skills, paying attention to body language, and increasing emotional intelligence can heighten our ability to empathize with others. Embracing our own vulnerability and exploring new perspectives can also help.

If you want to cultivate greater empathy, before anything else, you need to acknowledge your biases. We all have biases or prejudices toward individuals or groups, whether we are aware of it or not. Even though biases may arise frequently in personal interactions, these perceptions certainly are not the only reason people fail to understand one another. You can even misunderstand someone whose background is very similar to your own. Assume you don't know how the other person feels, because you probably don't. asking questions is the answer. Expressing a willingness to hear another's perspective will help that person feel respected. And once you have asked a question, be sure to really listen to what the other person has to say. While the person is speaking, make sure that you don't interrupt- allow the other person to finish speaking before you respond. If the person expresses negative emotions about a situation, avoid suggesting possible fixes unless he or she specifically requests your advice.

Empathy can motivate us to be good to others as we can imagine what it would be like to be in their position and think about how we would wish to be treated. Here, then, lies the origin of "The Golden Rule" of empathy. The Golden Rule can be expressed positively as: "treat others as you would like to be treated yourself." Hence, we should try to practice empathy for it is essential for building and maintaining relationships, as it helps us connect with others at a deeper level. It is also associated with higher self-esteem and life purpose.

Deciphering Concealed Characters

We humans, who are the most successful social animal on the planet are all consummate actors.

People generally tend to wear a mask that shows them in the best possible light- kind, confident, amiable. This invariably involves concealing their possible antagonistic feelings, their envy, their malice, their attempts at sabotaging others, and their intimidations. In the pursuit of life, we humans undeniably encounter people, who appear to possess quite empathetic traits that set them apart- they appear to possess atypical confidence, exceptional niceness and amiability, a great moral code of conduct, bewildering complacency, a menacing intellectual prowess. If we take these appearances for reality, we never really know their true feelings, and on occasion we are startled by sudden revelations of their clandestine hostility and nefariousness. Our task is to look past the distractions and become aware of their true character that leaks out of their masks, automatically at times. Once we learn to decipher and look through their disguises, we can train ourselves to adopt apt defensive measures.

If we try to delve deep into their temperament, we may notice a slight exaggeration to these traits, as they were masqueraded with sheer aptitude. The reality is that the empathetic trait is too exuberant not to conceal and distract the stumbling traits

With age, they try to polish and acuminate this public image. The underlying weakness is a key module of their shadow – something denied and suppressed. But, as human nature demonstrates, the deeper the suppression, the greater is the effervescence of the shadow. As they grow older and face adversities; at certain points of time their public image will begin to wane and their real self unclothe in forms of obsessions, ruthlessness, clandestine debasements and behaviour that is quite conflicting with their typical image.

Our task in order to decipher this shadow and bulwark ourselves from their detrimental effects; is simple: we just have to be frugal around those individuals who seem to exude such empathetic traits. It is very easy to get caught up in the appearance and first impression. We must gape at the emergence of the shadow over time. We must not let ourselves be intimidated by the show, but also be careful not to stir up their insecurities by appearing to mistrust their tall tales. In doing so, we become more authentic, exploiting to the maximum the energies we naturally possess to keep ourselves from stepping into deadly traps laid down by malevolent fraudsters. In the end, we will make our path more seamless by avoiding bewildering acts of sabotage.

In developing this particular skill, an understanding that will help us is that people's hostile actions never come out of the blue. There are always cues before they take any action.

Understanding and seeing through people's masks requires a amalgamation of emotional intelligence and observational skills.

The foremost step we need to take is to develop emotional intelligence by understanding our own emotions, motivations and biases. This self-awareness helps us relate to others on a deeper level. In order to experience empathy, we need to put ourselves into others' shoes and recognize the emotions they might be experiencing. This helps us decipher whether the presented emotions are genuine or a façade.

We must also be extra meticulous in observing non-verbal cues by paying attention to facial expressions, gesture, postures, and eye contact. Inconsistencies between verbal and non-verbal cues may indicate a mismatch between the expressed emotions and the true feelings. We also need to pay attention towards micro-expressions which are fleeting facial expressions lasting only a fraction of second which can reveal genuine emotions. Training ourselves to recognize micro-expressions can be valuable in seeing through masks.

Paying attention to how people speak- the tone, pitch and speed of speech, can also provide additional context to the words being spoken.

We need to be aware of sudden changes in behavioural patterns of individuals around us, as they might be harbingers of hidden malice or subdued vindictiveness.

Familiarizing and educating ourselves with psychological concepts such as cognitive dissonance, projection and defense mechanisms provide valuable insights, and hence can profoundly aid in deciphering underlying emotions.

Instead of just being a curious bystander, we have our part to play as well. While conversing with people, we need to make them feel safe and comforted by creating a warm environment. When people feel accepted, they are more likely to drop their masks. We should try to encourage people to share more about themselves for open-ended questions prompt deeper, more honest responses.

We should learn not to jump to conclusions by being open to understanding others' perspective and accepting that everyone has experiences that are unique to them and reasons for wearing masks.

We should bear in mind the fact that seeing through people's masks requires a combination of skills and deliberate practice; and that this practice should always be approached with understanding and due respect for others' boundaries.

Change Your Perspective of Death

Despite having cognizance of the truth that death is an inevitable part of life that we all must face, one of the most crippling intimidations we humans face is the fear of death. But this approach appears to be idiosyncratic and meaningless.

While it can be difficult to accept, acknowledging death as a natural part of life, will help us cultivate a deeper appreciation for the time we have with our loved ones, confront our own mortality, and live a more meaningful life. We should learn to draw a parallel between a routine journey of daily life and journey to death. A routine journey requires an individual to travel regularly from the safety of his home, across a threshold and into the unknown. Similarly the journey into death is beyond time and place to the unknown.

Death is like a vast ocean which is massive and difficult to comprehend. When the waves crash against the shore, they make a sound which is lively and intriguing. Similarly, we humans should accept imminent death calmly, without fear. There should not be any moaning, sorrow or lament to know the coming of death.

By associating ourselves with the reality of death, we associate more vividly and profoundly to the reality and ampleness of life. By repressing our awareness of it, we shift away from the reality of life. William Hazlitt rightly said, "Our repugnance to death increases in proportion to our consciousness of having lived in vain."

When we disconnect ourselves from the awareness of death, we develop a distended relationship with time: we come to imagine that we always have more time than is the reality. It is at this state of mind that we grow more and more familiar with procrastinations. If we have any plans or goals, more than often, we find it tough to commit ourselves to it with the dedication and zeal it requires. We experience a generalized anxiety, as we sense the urgency to get things done, and we find ourselves always postponing and scattering our forces. We have to awaken to the reality that time passes always much more quickly than we imagine and make it a continual meditation. We have to scrutinize our daily actions by drawing wisdom form this awareness of the brevity of life.

Then, if there is a deadline imposed upon us on a particular project, we experience a boost of energy; thereby committing more profoundly our mind and body to the purpose. This makes our work more creative and opens door to a relishing synchronisation of successes.

If we think of our mortality as such a kind of deadline, we give an effect similar to the aforementioned one to all our actions in life. When we keep in mind that our life is short, that it could end any day; we unconsciously experience a sensation of urgency to make the most of this limited time.

Life, as a matter of course, involves misery and pain. There is too much in life we cannot control, with death epitomising this. We will inevitably experience depression, agony, misery and physical illnesses. We will inevitably go through painful separations from people. We will face pain of defeat and betrayal. In the face of this grim reality, we have a choice: We can try to avoid these painful moments by distracting ourselves, by engaging ourselves sin indulgences or addictive behaviour and delving in the temporary relief yet devastation they offer. We can also lower our ambitions so that we do not expose ourselves to any form of failures or ridicule. If we do not get involved in any relationships we can avoid heart rending moments from the separation. But this approach towards life seems to be utmost unrealistic and impractical. In order to live a fulfilling life, we need to accept these adversities, and even embrace them, in order to enlighten ourselves with the encompassing lessons they offer. In doing so, we learn an important life skill of getting accustomed to some degree of physical or emotional pain. In the process, we strengthen ourselves and we affirm life itself, accepting all of it's possibilities; at the core of which is our complete acceptance of death.

Death is the greatest unknown, but the fear of dying should not be allowed to get so intense that it starts to interfere with our daily life and eclipses all other thoughts, impeding us from living a gratifying life.

The habit of thinking about dying instead of making the most of life, due, generally stems from lack of purpose or lack of a commodious occupation. This trepidation is more prevalent among the aged, but every so often, the more youthful fall prey to it. The greatest of all remedies for the fear of death is a burning desire for achievement, accompanied by ardent labour. A busy individual hardly finds leisure to ponder on death. He finds life too savouring to worry about dying. More than often, the fear of death is intimately entangled with the fear of poverty, where one's death would leave one's loved ones in a poverty-stricken, beleaguered state.

This terrifying fear of death can be overcome by focusing on making the most out of life. Marcus Aurelius observed, "It is not death that a man should fear, but he should fear never beginning to live."

If we do not want to enslave ourselves to our fears and trepidations, we need to live life to the fullest and experience a taste of true freedom that it accords. We need to be more daring without feeling afraid of the consequences. We always need to refrain ourselves from the addictions we foolishly employ to numb our anxiety. By getting directed this way, we commit utterly to our work, our relationships, to all our actions, and thus, live life to the fullest.

Acknowledgement

I am eternally indebted to my loving parents and my doting brother without whose unconditional love and support, I would have never dared to dream to find myself in the writing medium. I remain thankful to all nine of my four-legged babies for teaching me the meaning of selfless love and unquestioning loyalty. I am whole-heartedly grateful to my angel boy, Tom for always showering upon me his auspicious blessings from heaven.

And last but not the least, I would like to extend my gratitude towards public interaction and management team of "Blue Rose Publishers" for their sincere and valued guidance without which my book would not be brought about.

www.ingramcontent.com/pod-product-compliance
Lightning Source LLC
LaVergne TN
LVHW041544070526
838199LV00046B/1823